$500 EVERYDAY *with*
FACEBOOK FAN PAGES! *ver 1.8*

(Updated: 16th November 2010)

From the desk of your favorite author
Adam C. Miller
A member of Warrior Forum

DISCLAIMER

The information presented herein represents the views of the author as of the date of publication. Because of the rate with which conditions change, the author reserves the rights to alter and update his opinions based on the new conditions. This manual is for informational purposes only and the author does not accept any responsibilities for any liabilities resulting from the use of this information. While every attempt has been made to verify the information provided here, the author and his referrals cannot assume any responsibility for errors, inaccuracies or omissions. Any slights of people or organizations are unintentional.

This publication is not intended for use as any source of advice such as legal, medical, or accounting. The publisher wants to stress that the information contained herein may be subject to varying international, federal, state, and/or local laws or regulations. The purchaser or reader of this publication assumes responsibility for the use of these materials and information. Adherence to all applicable laws and regulations, including international, federal, state and local governing professional licensing, business practices, advertising, and all other aspects of doing business in the EU, US, Canada or any other jurisdiction is the sole responsibility of the purchaser or reader. Neither the author nor the publisher assume any responsibility or liability whatsoever on the behalf of the purchaser or reader of these materials. Any perceived slight of any individual or organization is purely unintentional.

This book is for personal use only. It should serve as a reference only with no guarantee to any personal or financial gains. Results from usage of materials described in this book varies. By reading this material, you agree that the author is not liable on any consequences arising from usage of this book.

Congratulations!

Now, you <u>DO HAVE</u> resale rights.

You can sell this report for a price,

give away or distribute this report as a bonus or

as a free gift to your subscribers.

Please Remember, You do NOT have any right to edit this report.

Hello again, I am **Adam C. Miller** from United Kingdom. I am a reputed member at Warrior Forum. Thousands of people on the internet know me for publishing internet marketing e-books which are the MOST REALISTIC ONES. I never hurry while publishing an e-book. I do research, find new methods, apply them, and if I am successful, I tell others in my e-books. You can say that I write an e-book once in 6 months, but it is always **the best one**. You might have read my other e-books earlier too, so here is another one. I hope you will like it as much as you liked my previous e-books. This e-book has a version i.e. 1.8 and if I have some updates on this method, I will put it in the next version of this e-book.

If you have any doubts regarding this method or you face any problem then you can contact me at GetAllDetails@yahoo.com Please mention the name of the e-book while contacting, otherwise, I will be unable to know about which method you want my help.

Note: All screenshots in this e-book are in high resolution, please use latest version of Adobe Reader to view this file. Moreover, The screenshots in this e-book are updated TILL **16th November 2010**. If you want to see the latest screenshots, then just message me on the forum or send me an email.

Thanks

Adam C. Miller

Let's Start...

You read many e-books on making money, but <u>NO E-BOOK</u> gives you any guarantee that you will make money using its method. But, here is the MOST REALISTIC AND PRACTICAL e-book, you have ever read, in your life. It is a blueprint of making <u>ROCK SOLID INCOME</u> consistently, <u>WITHOUT</u> missing even a single day!

It is an exact form of a method, I use for getting <u>500 UNIQUE VISITORS DAILY</u> to my website and making $500 PER DAY, $3500 PER WEEK or say $15000 PER MONTH. This is the most recent e-book from my desk and is written in February, 2010. I have reached at this level of $500 EVERYDAY in 30 DAYS ONLY, starting from ZERO! But, if you want to make $500 today only, then this e-book is NOT for you, because my method will take few days.

Everyone can make money from its website, if it gets traffic. If you already have a website, then to make money, you need a lot of traffic! So, first of all, let's decide from where you can get the traffic. The best source of getting traffic are the Search Engines (SEs). But is it easy to see your website on the #1 page of <u>Google</u>? I will like to do efforts for it, but it will take that much long time, that I may leave internet marketing, being disappointed. Should you go for <u>Google Adwords?</u> Well! I am not lucky in using Google Adwords, as it took all cash from my pockets and I got no sales from it for 2 months continuously. Many people may have become successful with it, but, I was NOT. So, what is the solution? The next best place for getting traffic is <u>Social Networking Websites</u>. I believe on <u>Facebook</u> for getting targeted traffic, as it is **#1** Social Networking Website with 300 MILLION active users and every user has <u>more than 100 friends</u> at an average. So, don't you think that this can be a major source of traffic among all social networking websites? The best source of traffic from Facebook are its fan pages.

A successful <u>Fan Page</u> can bring:

- Regular

- Targeted

- Highly interested

- Easily convertible

- Most suitable

...traffic to your website that <u>WILL BUY</u> your product!

Here I am going to tell you, how to make an <u>ULTIMATE FAN PAGE</u> that adds <u>200 more fans</u> to it automatically everyday, and brings <u>IMMENSE TRAFFIC TO YOUR WEBSITE!</u> & let you make <u>$500 EVERYDAY.</u> My fan page brings thousands of <u>Targeted Visitors</u> to my website every month and load my pockets with money <u>WITHOUT ANY EXTRA EFFORT</u>!

I created a new Facebook account <u>just 30 days</u> ago & these are the stats of this account:

****

Total Friends:	4577
Total Fans:	More than 55000
UVs to my website from this fan page:	500-600 Per Day
Average Sales:	15-20 Per Day
Average Income:	$450-$600 Per Day

(As my website design is very poor and not convincing, that's why my conversion rate (rate at which visitors are converted into customers) is 2%-3% only, I am trying to improve it more and I hope I will be able to take it to 4%-5% easily that will double my sales.)

****

I will surely show you the screenshots of my Facebook account and fan page. Not only this, you will also see the traffic stats, and my income proofs, in the next pages, so keep reading... ☺

Now, you might be thinking that if I am boasting that much, then why I don't share the url of my fan page? The reason is that I do not want to be on a risk of my fan page being reported by anyone, because I am making great from this. I know if only few people report a fan page then Facebook will remove it without even investigating. On the other hand, if you really want traffic to your website & want to make $500 EVERYDAY, then you should either trust me or you can close this e-book and start reading another one that claims making $$$$$ per day or some impossible IDIOT FIGURES! Ok, Let's start learning, making an ULTIMATE FAN PAGE on Facebook that brings HUGE TRAFFIC to your website and let you make **$500 EVERYDAY!**

First of all, Create a new GMAIL account. Yes! Only Gmail email account should be there. Now, create a new Facebook account, as some risk of being banned is there so you should create a new Facebook Account and should NOT use the existing one. Use your new Gmail email account to create this new Facebook account, I will let you know later, why? If you want to get some crazy traffic then you should make a profile with a girl's name. Name should be a sweet one. The profile should look genuine. Goto http://www.images.google.com and find the things that represent girls like, flowers, clothes, some romantic colors etc. and add it as a picture on your profile. I do NOT recommend placing a picture of someone other. Because, it may put adverse affect on that person image and you may be in trouble for that.

Enter as much information as you can. People do not like empty profiles. After you have created a new Facebook Account, it is the time to start adding friends to it. Remember, do NOT make a fan page until you have proper number of friends. You can add maximum of 5000 friends to your Facebook a/c. First of all, your motive should be to exploit this opportunity. **Remember,** this is the most important task. All of your website traffic, income, success etc. depends upon it. Generally, adding 5000 friends may take ages, but you will see, how you can add 5000 friends to your Facebook account in 7 days only, using my technique.

I am going to tell you a formula THAT IS UNBEATABLE! About 400-600 people will be joining you daily, WITHOUT FAILURE!

I am going to describe each and everything about this method, so slowly, that you will love it. I will show you how SIMPLE it is to get 5000 friends in 7 Days Only and make a fan page that brings ultimate traffic to your website. Keep reading patiently… ☺

Facebook allows you to use your email account to find, whether people in your email account, are on Facebook or not? If they are on Facebook, then you can add them as friends. But, you do not have even a single contact in your Gmail account, because it is a new account. Now, we need a lot of contacts in our email account so that we can use those contacts to find, invite and add people on Facebook. We need a huge email list now. What will you do in this case, either you purchase email lists or you build an opt-in list yourself. But, it will take months to get a large email list and the worst thing is that if you are going to buy an email list then you will have to pay $400-$1000 for it. Further, there is no guarantee that it will work or not. Now, if I suggest you to buy an email list paying $500 to a webmaster then you will surely like to kick me hard. The only alternative that is available at this time is an email extractor.

***** STOP! Don't think that I am going to sell you an email extractor… LOL… This is not a crapy e-book that contains affiliate links from Clickbank or Commission Junction websites to make sales. I am making a FIVE FIGURES income monthly from my own website, so, few cents from affiliate commission will not change my life. ☺

****

Have you ever used an email extractor? An email extractor harvests email IDs from the internet and gives you an email list containing those collected IDs. *But, Is it advisable to use email IDs harvested by an email extractor to invite people?* There are many disadvantages of using an email extractor. First of all, email extractor extracts same email IDs from the internet, every time you use it. Second thing is that there are email IDs of companies, and other business houses that are of NO use to you. Simply, you are NOT willing to send an invitation to a mobile phone selling company at its email ID to join you on Facebook... LOL. How silly, it will be! ☺

The final alternative is an email IDs/list generator. Email IDs/list generators are very different from email extractors, as they generate supposed email IDs using common names of the people. These email IDs belong to general public and not to the companies, firms or business houses. These kinds of generators are the recent blessing to the internet marketers. There are a lot of email list generators available on the internet that can generate thousands of email IDs in a short time. The best thing is that you can use different combinations of the names, different settings, different domain selection etc. to produce THOUSANDS OF UNIQUE EMAIL IDS everyday.

I found few of email list generators on the internet which are listed below:-

- Emailsmartz email generator

- Fast Email IDs generator

- Acute Email IDs Production Engine

- SharkGen E-mail Generator

You can select any of the above softwares. But I recommend Acute Email IDs Production Engine available in the list above. (Most of you will think, I am pushing this software to you... LOL) There are so many reasons behind it. First, I found it the cheapest one in price, but still very effective and good in quality and second, it's very quick to install & easy to use, and their support is also very good. Although, it cost me few $$ but, it has already paid 5000 times of its cost back to me in shape of sales of my product. Yes! I have recovered 5000 times of its cost. It all depends upon you, which software to choose. But, if you test other softwares too then please send me a review of them, so that I can add their features too, when I publish an update of this e-book in the next version.

The best advantage of using email IDs generators that more than 70% of email IDs actually exist. Means, if you have generated 4000 email IDs then 2800 will be working ones and this is a fantastic figure. If you use software more diligently and use most common people names, most common domains and most common settings then the success rate is 80% or more, read their help book first before using it.

Use your email IDs/list generator, there must be an option to **save/export** email IDs in a **text file** in the software you use, otherwise, we can't fulfill our purpose.

Ok, This is the most simple but important task. Produce near about 1000 email IDs, and **save/export** them in a **text file**, it will take only 5 minutes of yours. Now, open **MS_Excel** (any version) and make two headings in a new file. First column with heading 'Names' and second column with heading 'Email ID' as shown in the picture below.

	A	B	C
1	Name	Email ID	
2			
3			
4			
5			

Copy all email IDs from the **text file** (use ctrl+A to select all) and **paste** them under heading 'Email ID' in excel.

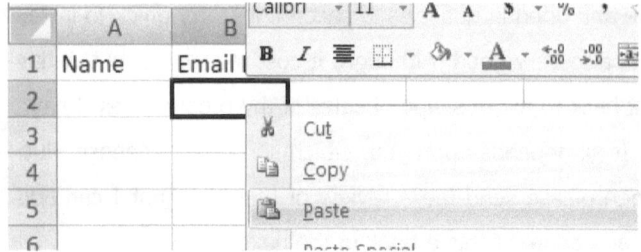

You can leave the Column 'Name' as blank.

Your excel file will look as below:

Save this file choosing Save as type as '*CSV (Comma Delimited)*' as shown in the picture below:

File name:	4000_Email_IDs	
Save as type:	CSV (Comma delimited)	

Save   Cancel

Congratulations! You have successfully made a *CSV File* containing thousands of email IDs in it. **Was it difficult?** I guess NOT. Your 60% work is complete now. If you have successfully saved a contact file (.CSV) in the format I mentioned, then you are VERY CLOSE to $500 EVERYDAY. You can create as many *contact files (.CSV)* as you want by producing different email IDs and pasting them in excel files. You may find this process a little boring, but remember your goal.

<u>$500 EVERYDAY IS NOT A SMALL AMOUNT!</u>

Keep yourself motivated! Just imagine about the things you have only desired of, but could not get them. Now, it is the time to buy those things. ☺

1. Now, open your new Gmail account and click on contacts.

2. Click on **import,** you will find it in the right side, top corner.

3. Browse the CSV file and click Import.

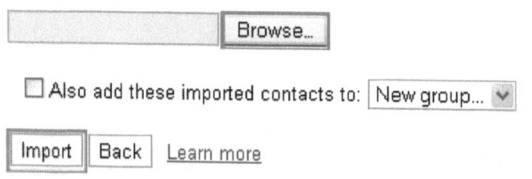

Import

We support importing CSV files from Outlook, Outlook Express, Y;
vCard from apps like Apple Address Book.

Please select a CSV or vCard file to upload:

[   ] [Browse...]

☐ Also add these imported contacts to: [New group... ▼]

[Import] [Back] Learn more

4. You will see soon that the email IDs from that CSV file has been imported in your Gmail account. Look, I have imported 2413 email IDs in few seconds.

Import

We have imported all **2413** contacts found in the uploaded file.

8 contacts from the uploaded file have been merged with contacts already in your Google address book.
Details...

[OK] Learn more

5. Do this process again and again by making new CSV files as I mentioned above. This is a little boring task but if you can not spend few minutes then you have no right to make thousands of dollars. When you will upload 2-3 CSV files and your Gmail account will have 9000-10000 contacts in it, you will get a message that Gmail can not import more contacts, as your address book is full.

6. Look, I have imported total <u>9620 contacts</u> in my Gmail account and address book is full.

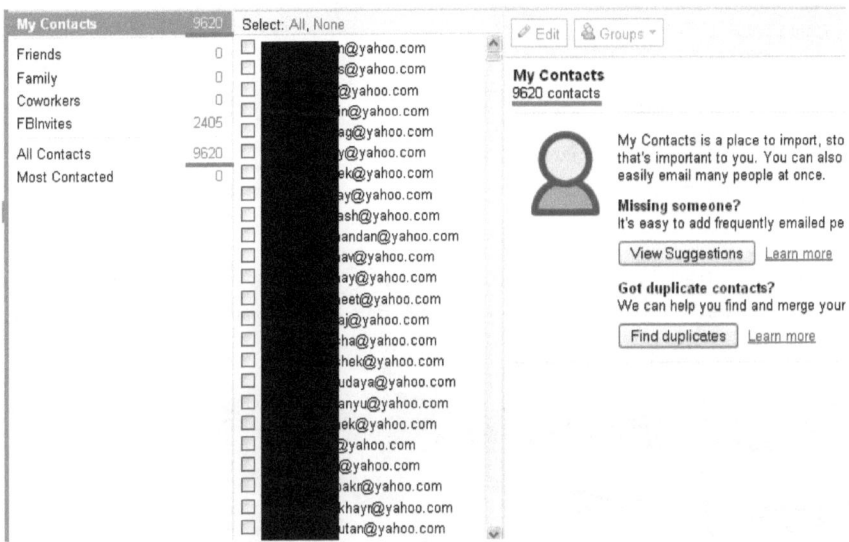

7. Now visit your Facebook home page, and then click on **Friends,** this option is available in left side menu. You will see the window shown below.

** Facebook keep on changing its interface. You may do some research in case you do not find an option.

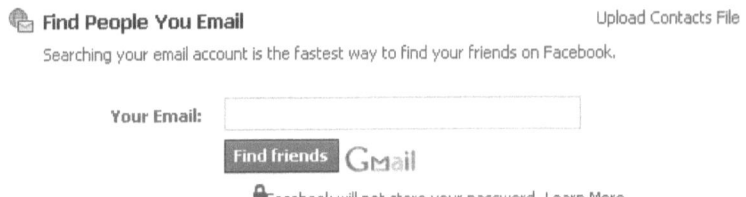

8. Enter your Gmail account and then click on Find Friends. It will ask for a username and password, if you are not logged in to your Gmail account. Enter your login

details. If you are already logged in your Gmail account, then it will not ask for a username and password. Then, It will ask your permission to allow or not. Click on Allow.

- Google Contacts

☑ Remember this approval

You can always change your Google Account approval settings. Facebook.com is not owned, operated, or controlled by Google or its owners. Learn more

9. Soon you will see that Facebook is importing your contacts and finding friends on Facebook using your contacts in Gmail. It may take few minutes, have patience.

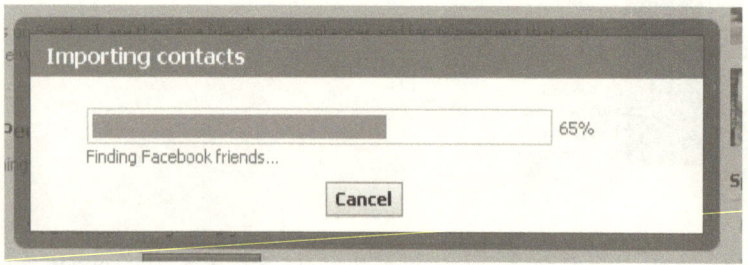

10. After importing your Gmail contacts, Facebook will show you the people who are on Facebook from those contacts.

Look, Facebook imported my all 9620 contacts from Gmail account and found that 334 out of those are already on Facebook. You know, what does it mean? It means, I can send a friend request to 334 PEOPLE in a SINGLE STROKE and AUTOMATICALLY !

It is really a VERY POWERFUL METHOD!

Now, the RAPID PROCESS of adding friends has begin my friend!

VOILA! It means at this pace, soon I will reach 5000 friends level....

IMPORTANT: There is a limit on the number of contacts you can import in Gmail. It is around 9000-10000 as I told earlier. You can not import more contacts. So, you have two options:

1. Create few gmail accounts and import CSV files to them and use them to invite people on Facebook by logging in to each email account one by one.

2. Once you invite people on Facebook, delete all contacts from your email account and then import fresh CSV files to add new contacts in it.

I was using <u>Acute Email IDs Production Engine</u> for this purpose and it is really like a factory for generating email IDs, although it does not verify email IDs but it all depends upon you how to use it to get maximum.

If you face any problem in this importing process, feel free to mail me at <u>GetAllDetails@yahoo.com</u>

After sending friend requests to Facebook users, next window will now show the contacts that are NOT on Facebook. You should <u>NOT</u> send request to them. Skip that process. Again, click on 'Friends' in the left side menu and repeat the same process to find more friends and add them.

Follow this practice, ONLY TWO TIMES a day importing 3-4 *contact file (CSV)* in Gmail at a time, containing a good number of email IDs and then inviting them on Facebook. Your software will take only 2 minutes to generate email IDs. Yes! I know, it is a little boring process, but *No pains, No gains, My Friend!*

Your chances of being successful are very high... because...

A lot of lazy people are there who will NOT take action on this report, so this thing is beneficial for you. Because when less people will act on this report, your chances to grab this opportunity are more. So DON'T GIVE UP!!

I am going to share with you the screenshots of my Facebook Profile, Traffic Figures and Income Statements *plus*, I am going to tell you about creating a Fan Page that brings <u>INSANE TRAFFIC</u> to my website, in the next few pages. So, keep on reading...

You know, Facebook activities GO VIRAL! When you will start adding some friends, their friends will also send you the friend requests. Your work is just to accept those invitations. See, how many invitations I got after one hour I sent first invitation.

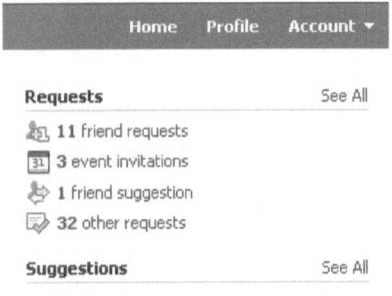

I was having more than ***95 friends*** *after an hour of sending invitations,* on the VERY FIRST DAY! I know, this figure is unbelievable! BUT, IT IS REAL!

After 5 hours, I was having near about 200 friends. I used only 5-6 contact file (CSV) and got that amount of friends. Make sure that your email IDs generator/software should be a quick one so that you need not to waste time in making new contact file (CSV).

This was the 2ND Day. I used 3 more contact files (CSV) in my other Gmail accounts and use them on Facebook to invite people. At an average, creation of contact file (CSV), importing in Gmail account and then using it on Facebook was taking only 10 minutes of mine. Means, I was spending only one hour daily for this work.

On late evening, I checked my profile and I had more than 600 friends.

I was keeping screenshot everyday, because, I am an active member at <u>Digital point</u> <u>forum</u>, too. I was sharing my progress in <u>this thread</u>. But, the thread was deleted by moderators, because, It got some sort of racial discussion by the DigitalPoint (DP) members.

Now, I was getting 100-150 requests per day and I was making numerous friends daily. I took this screenshot on my 3rd day. Look how many people have become my friends. Note one thing, that my friend requests and additions are being multiplied, every day.

DAY-3

DAY-5

DAY-6

I was accepting near about 150-200 Friend requests daily and sending near about 400-500 friend requests. Now, you will say that Facebook does not allow you to send 20 or more friend requests, manually.

But, when you invite them from you email ID, this limit does not work ☺

Look at the picture of my wall, this was the daily picture of my wall.

This was the 7th Day and I reached at 5000 Friends level !

I was just <u>one friend short</u> of the limit! ... LOL

Friends

4,999 friends   See All

Once you reach at this stage, your <u>80% work</u> is complete.

Now, you have seen, how easy it is to reach 5000 friends level. BUT, I WILL NOT BE ON THE REST, UNTIL I ACHIEVE MY TARGET. Once you have reached 5000 friends level, now, it is a PERFECT TIME to <u>create your fan page</u>. This fan page will bring HUNDREDS OF VISITORS TO YOUR WEBSITE EVERYDAY! Not only this, as the number of fans will increase, <u>more fans</u> will keep on adding at a rapid speed. According to my experience daily <u>200 NEW</u> users will become fan of your fan page and will be visiting to your website.

How to create a fan page that spreads on Facebook like a forest fire!

First of all, think, which product/service/CPA offer/Affiliate program or anything you want to promote? I have not joined any CPA offer yet in my life. I am having a website, where I sell <u>weight lose product</u>. My purpose is to sell an e-book that contains a course that will help to lose weight and you will look slim and fit. So, my purpose is to gain attention of the people who want to be slim or want to be fit. So I will name my fan page as:

'Fitness House', 'Get-Set-Slim-Go', 'I want to be slim', 'weight lose mantra' or 'Crazy for fitness' etc.

Remember, that your fan page will appear in search engines too, so make sure you use your keywords in the name of your fan page.

To create a new page, click on 'Ads and pages' option available on your home page in the left side. (Facebook keeps on changing its layout so, if you do not find an option where I mention in this report then just do some research. Use Google to find any option in Facebook.)

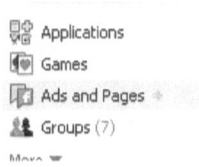

Then click on 'Create a new page'

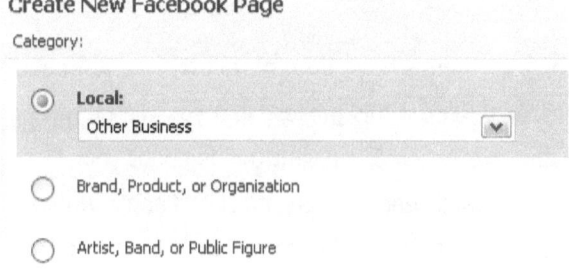

Fill all the possible details etc. in your fan page. If you add a picture to your fan page then it would look more attractive. You can download a good image from a free image download websites. Make sure that you are NOT breaking any copyright or trademark laws using a picture. Better, if you can create your own. You can visit google images to get an idea. If you find anything deficit in your Fan page then first, complete it, before asking friends to join it.

NOTE: Make sure that you have inserted a link to your website in your Fan Page. It should be your own website, because, you will need to verify it later on.

Now, it's the time to tell people about your Fan Page. To suggest this page to your friends, use the option 'suggest to friends' available on your page.

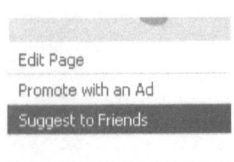

You can select all of your friends and can suggest this fan page. Believe me, if you send request to 500 people only then you will be having 5000 or more fans in 5-6 days only, if you work properly.

How, it will happen?

When you see that many of your friends have become fan of your fan page, ask them to suggest this page to their friends. Repeat this process and you will be having tremendous growth. If you keep on posting interesting & relevant things about your niche on your fan page then it will be indexed in search engine, very quickly. People who are making searches in your niche, will find it interesting and will become fan of it, even if they are not in your friend list. Great! Now you are receiving SE traffic too, now.

You know, when I was having near about 5000 friends and I suggested my page to my friends then on the NEXT DAY ONLY, I got more than 138 MESSAGES from different people who said that THEY LIKED MY FAN PAGE!

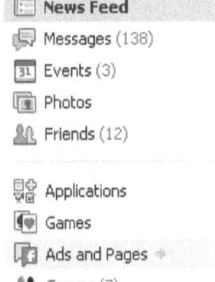

News Feed
Messages (138)
Events (3)
Photos
Friends (12)

Applications
Games
Ads and Pages
Groups (7)

At a **5000 Friends Level** when your friends become fan of your page, it is posted on their walls and their friends will also like to see your page and then their friends too... and so on... Your work is to just wait and watch now! Just see how quickly, near about 200-250 more people are becoming fan of your page, EVERDAY!

But, remember, your first work is to add 5000 friends. *Make it your Passion! If you can not add 5000 friends, you should not dream about this success!*

In 7 Days I added 5000 friends and when I created my Fan page ON **8TH DAY** and *suggested it to my friends* I got **60 Fans** within 2-3 hours.

Fans
6 of 61 fans   See All

DAY – 9 (Next day after creation of my fan page, see the viral growth! It is RAPID!)

Fans
6 of 1,800 fans   See All

DAY - 10

Fans	
6 of 3,736 fans	See All

DAY – 13 (I got tremendous growth in few days, Now, I know how Facebook works virally!)

Fans	
6 of 8,111 fans	See All

DAY-17

Fans	
6 of 13,127 fans	See All

DAY-19

Fans	
6 of 16,270 fans	See All

DAY-22

Fans	
6 of 21,771 fans	See All

DAY-25

Fans	
6 of 31,714 fans	See All

DAY-27

Fans
6 of 38,887 fans   See All

DAY - 29

Fans
6 of 46,971 fans   See All

On 30TH DAY, I had <u>more than 50000 Fans</u>.

Fans
6 of 52,465 fans   See All

You might have noticed the <u>HUGE JUMPS</u> in the number of fans, between days. The real reason of this speed is that because if my every friend has near about 100 friends at an average, it means, my page was viewed by 5000 X 100 = 500000 People, on the day, when I shared it. I could not get this amount of fans, if I have shared this page with only 100-150 friends.

When you reach at 50,000 or more level, it is AUTOPILOT! Now, you should not think more about gaining fans, because near about 200-250 more people will be joining you, daily. At this time, you have GOLD IN YOUR HANDS!!! Now it is the time to use this traffic. Start posting status updates about your website as soon as you have 10000 fans. 2-3 updates per day will be enough. I posted my health tips, diet information, slimming tactics and all other relevant things with MY WEBSITE LINK. I asked my fans to visit my site and check new health, fitness and slimming methods.

I am too bad in writing posts and updates and 99% people ignore me. They either do not read status updates or do not visit my website. But, still from 50000 fans I am getting <u>500 VISITORS EVERYDAY!!</u> (i.e. 1% remaining people). Look at the increase in traffic since; I started using Facebook Fan Page.

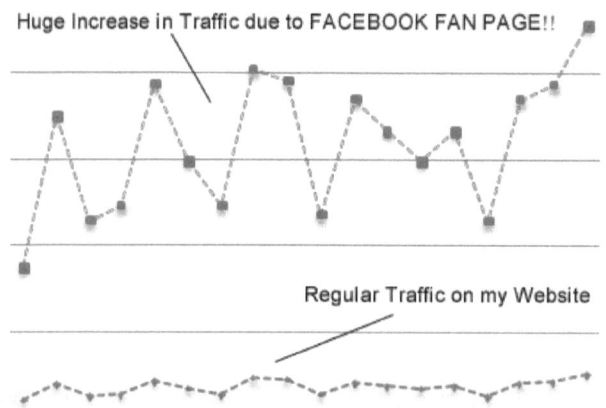

From 30TH DAY, I was getting near about 500-600 UVs everyday from Facebook Fan Page Only. Now as a webmaster you know that <u>minimum conversion rate</u> for an average website is only 3%-5%, I mentioned in the beginning that, I am planning to improve my website look and will make it more attractive and convincing to get more sales. On 5% conversion rate if you are getting only 500 UVs per day, even then you are making <u>16-20 SALES DAILY!</u> This is the same output that I am getting from Facebook Fan Page.

Yes! I am getting <u>15-16 sales</u> everyday (at an average)

and price of my product is $29.99 !!

This is the latest screenshot of my Gmail account,

You can check, there are <u>TONS OF EMAILS</u> from E-junkie showing MASSIVE sales.

I have taken this screenshot on <u>16th November 2010 i.e. Today</u>

Inbox	E-junkie Notification - Sale [2010-11-16 19:32:46] -	... Transaction ID: 49L59352RT982813D Invoice: 1mc7d9j38		Nov 16
Inbox	E-junkie Notification - Sale [2010-11-16 18:50:58] -	... Transaction ID: 15A20475MV4225(Invoice: 1mc7d9fc		Nov 16
Inbox	E-junkie Notification - Sale [2010-11-16 17:04:50] -	... Transaction ID: 8HY666102031638 Invoice: 1mc7d9e		Nov 16
Inbox	E-junkie Notification - Sale [2010-11-16 16:23:36] -	... Transaction ID: 56N90543SV167231V Invoice: 1mc7		Nov 16
Inbox	E-junkie Notification - Sale [2010-11-16 14:18:28] -	... Transaction ID: 6DM937126U645921U Invo		Nov 16
Inbox	E-junkie Notification - Sale [2010-11-16 13:39:20] -	... Transaction ID: 0GW814938J05849		Nov 16
Inbox	E-junkie Notification - Sale [2010-11-16 08:01:05] -	... Transaction ID: 30N16139		Nov 16
Inbox	E-junkie Notification - Sale [2010-11-16 08:01:05] -	... Transaction ID:	15X Invoice: 1mc7d9fc	Nov 16
Inbox	E-junkie Notification - Sale [2010-11-16 05:27:24] -	... Transa	dR751853V Invoice: 1mc7d9e	Nov 16
Inbox	E-junkie Notification - Sale [2010-11-16 03:46:19] -	...	U72494FN806590P Invoice: 1mc7d9e	Nov 16
Inbox	E-junkie Notification - Sale [2010-11-16 02:47	...	tion ID: 4PW69973RJ3328540 Invoice: 1mc7d9e	Nov 16
Inbox	E-junkie Notification - Sale [2010-11-16 00:43:1	... Transaction ID: 46U11667LT690971U Invoice: 1mc7d9e1		Nov 16
Inbox	E-junkie Notification - Sale [2010-11-16 00:20:50] -	... Transaction ID: 8NC41462E5423620K Invoice: 1mc7d9d:		Nov 16

I can stretch this screenshot as long as I want, but to keep the file size small, I have taken a small screenshot of everything.

If you still do not believe then you can check the screenshot of my PayPal account at the next page.

Here is the **LATEST Screenshot** of my Paypal Account, showing MASSIVE sales.

This is not only the one day, this is my everyday story!! ☺

	Date		Type	Name/Email	Payment status	Details	Order status/Actions	Gross
☐	16-Nov-2010	🚩	Payment From		Completed	Details		$29.99
☐	16-Nov-2010		Payment From		Completed	Details		$29.99
☐	16-Nov-2010		Payment From		Completed	Details		$29.99
☐	16-Nov-2010		Payment From		Completed	Details		$29.99
☐	16-Nov-2010		Payment From		Completed	Details		$29.99
☐	16-Nov-2010		Payment From		Completed	Details		$29.99
☐	16-Nov-2010		Payment From		Completed	Details		$29.99
☐	16-Nov-2010		Payment From		Completed	Details		$29.99
☐	16-Nov-2010		Payment From		Completed	Details		$29.99
☐	16-Nov-2010		Payment From		Completed	Details		$29.99
☐	16-Nov-2010		Payment From		Completed	Details		$29.99
☐	16-Nov-2010		Payment From		Completed	Details		$29.99
☐	16-Nov-2010		Payment From		Completed	Details		$29.99
☐	16-Nov-2010		Payment From		Completed	Details		$29.99
☐	16-Nov-2010		Payment From		Completed	Details		$29.99

15-16 sales @ $29.99 is making me $450 - $500 DAILY !!

I am getting this success at a beginner's level. I have **_50000 Fans_** only and still making $500 PER DAY. Every week, I am getting more fans, more traffic and more sales. As you know, I am getting only 1% visitors to my website from my Facebook fan page but, what if you get 3% or 4% visitors? It means you will be getting 1500-2000 LASER TARGETED visitors to your website who are highly interested in your products and what if you are selling products at a higher price like $50?

Suppose, you can attract only 2% fans (*out of your 50000*) to your website and your conversion rate is only 3% and you have a product worth $50.

Your MINIMUM revenue:

50000 X 2% = 1000 visitors X 3% = 30 sales X $50 = **$1500 PER DAY !!**

But! You will not make any money by ONLY reading this e-book. You will have to act upon it. ☺

Now, if you do not have any product to sell, then you can promote others' product. Visit google and type 'Affiliate Programs' OR 'Cost Per Action Programs' OR 'Earn With CPA'

Here, I am giving few names of the networks where you can find products to promote and you can make HUGE commissions.

www.clickbank.com

www.cj.com

www.neverblue.com

www.maxbounty.com

www.affiliate.com

Visit those sites and sign up as an affiliate and start making commission offering their products to your Facebook friends or fans. Read their terms and conditions carefully before joining. You can simply push gaming, music, dating sites offers to Facebook Friends and can get huge money from the companies working as their affiliates. There are a lot of companies who pays you when someone referred by you, just enter its email ID on companies website or complete free offers. It is called 'email submit or zip submit programs'. Visit Google to find such programs.

There are a lot of opportunities to make money on Facebook. You can make money by selling your own product, service, desigining work, ebooks etc. OR you can join CPA networks, work as an affiliate or sell other products for a commission.

BUT, it is possible only when you have a large number of Facebook friends. After you reach at 5000 FB friends level, you can do anything and earn any amount, and with this method you can achieve this target in *__7 days only !__*

How to avoid getting banned on Facebook?

Most of the users show a lot of excitement and invite thousands of people on the same day. Doing this will result in BAN at Facebook. Facebook will disable your account, if you do it rapidly. I added 5000 friends in 7 days, it may take 12-13 days, if you do it. So, do not get panic.

Do not commit mistakes that can lead to a BAN.

Here are few tips to avoid being banned:

1. Use a sweet girl profile. Age should be from 21-29. Acceptance ratio of a girls request is higher than a male one. Use a name from your native country or the country you want to target.

2. *Do not add* more than 300-400 friends a day. Do not forget, people will also send you the friend requests. As soon as you will be sending friends requests and will be making new friends you will also be getting more and more friends requests. So, it will speed up the work.

3. Do not *send* invitations to those who are not on Facebook, means do not send email invites.

4. If someone ask you 'Do you know me?' or 'Do we know each other?' then tell him/her "I am a new comer to the Facebook and liked your profile that's why I send you a friend request. Can we become friends?" You will get great response.

So, what do you think now? You have seen WITH PROOFS, how easy it is to start getting ULTIMATE TRAFFIC from Facebook fan pages.

Still, there will be so many people who will think about it a lot! Many people will be there, who will be checking the screenshots in this e-book closely to find out the mistakes, so that they can tell others that these are not real... LOL... This is a common practice, because, many people make filthy reports to gain their commissions by making some sales, from affiliate sites. Due to these unwanted writers, people generally do not believe on genuine reports, too. Even if you do not trust me, then it will not affect me!

Because, tomorrow, I will be making another $500 sitting in my room and most of you might be reading another e-book for *getting rich quickly!*

Think out of the box, Get out of the crowd, be the different and let the world know about you! *TAKE ACTION!*

Let me know your feedback about this report!

Doubts? Mail me at GetAllDetails@yahoo.com

Click here to watch video tutorial to learn this method in action and make

5000 Facebook Friends in 7 Days!

& Start Making

$500 Everyday!

ALL THE BEST!

Thanks for your time!

Your Friend,

- Adam C. Miller